1,000,000 Books

are available to read at

---◇---

www.ForgottenBooks.com

---◇---

Read online
Download PDF
Purchase in print

ISBN 978-0-243-25728-7
PIBN 10748673

1 MONTH OF
FREE
READING

at
www.ForgottenBooks.com

By purchasing this book you are eligible for one month membership to ForgottenBooks.com, giving you unlimited access to our entire collection of over 1,000,000 titles via our web site and mobile apps.

To claim your free month visit:
www.forgottenbooks.com/free748673

English
Français
Deutsche
Italiano
Español
Português

www.forgottenbooks.com

Mythology Photography **Fiction**
Fishing Christianity **Art** Cooking
Essays Buddhism Freemasonry
Medicine **Biology** Music **Ancient
Egypt** Evolution Carpentry Physics
Dance Geology **Mathematics** Fitness
Shakespeare **Folklore** Yoga Marketing
Confidence Immortality Biographies
Poetry **Psychology** Witchcraft
Electronics Chemistry History **Law**
Accounting **Philosophy** Anthropology
Alchemy Drama Quantum Mechanics
Atheism Sexual Health **Ancient History**
Entrepreneurship Languages Sport
Paleontology Needlework Islam
Metaphysics Investment Archaeology
Parenting Statistics Criminology
Motivational

The Christian Sun

J. O. Atkinson, Editor.   Price, $1.50 a Year.

Vol. 64.   GREENSBORO, N. C., FEBRUARY 14, 1912.   No. 7.

TRUST.

BY THE REV. A. J. CHAPMAN.

Beside my baby's crib at night, I lay upon my bed;
My little one could hear the storm, and feared the dark,
   she said.
The night was dark, the clouds were low, the storm's voice
   sounded wild,
So baby heart craved some one near, lest danger meet the
   child.
Yet not content, my baby girl, for me just near to linger,
Her tiny hand stole out the bed and clasped around my
   finger.
I could not chide, refuse her plaint, be hardened to her
   tears;
She understood not reasons why, so I must soothe her fears.
I, too, a child about to rest, my play and cares aside,
Can ask no dearer, sweeter boon than near Thee to abide.
The night is dark, the clouds are low, the storm to me is
   wild,
For I, too, know not reasons why, since I am but Thy child.
My life, O Father, in Thy hand, may little be or much;
But I, Thy child, shall be content, if I may feel Thy touch.
Thou'lt not withhold Thy care by night, by day Thy Help
   divine;
And dark or cloud or storm are naught—my hand shall
   rest in thine.   —In N. Y. Advocate.

ORGAN OF THE SOUTHERN CHRISTIAN CONVENTION.

3

EDITORIAL.

REPENT.

(Repent ye; for the kingdom of heaven is at hand. Mt. 3: 2. Golden text for Sun..ay,. February 18).

The Bible is one loud, long call to man to repent. The Old Testament opens and closes with it; the New is writ large with it. from the first to the last chapter. In Genesis God is seeking Adam, and walking in the Garden saying, "Adam, where art thou?" A call to repentance. Malachi closes the Old Testament with a paragraph beginning, "Remember ye the law of Moses my servant * * * lest I come and smite the earth with a curse." A call to repentance. Matthew begins the New Testament with the biography of a great and good man whose one message was, "Repent, Repent, Repent." This is the message of John. And that of Jesus is no less distinct, and His theme is the same. And Revelation sounds the same predominant note, "The Spirit and the bride say, Come." Man is afar off because of sin and God is calling him to repentance. We say then that the plea of the Book of God is, Repent.

And this was needed and is needed, for man is ever sinning and falling away from God. Repentance is that act where by man having discovered his aloofness from God, makes effort to get back to God. "You cannot be sure that you are perfectly saved till you know. you are utterly lost." When one realizes that one is lost just then and there the act of repentance begins' "Penitence is being sorry enough to quit,.' said a little girl, and only needs this to complete it: "and willingness to ask God to help you quit and keep you quit."

This was John's message. He saw a whole generation of men and women walking in their evil and perverse ways, and he called on them to quit, and to face about.

John is one of the truly great men of history. He had a mission and gave himself unflinchingly to its performance. He had a message and he gave himself without fear or favor to its utterance. And the greatness of the man is measured by the tremendousness of his message. You can tell a great man by the greatness of his message. John had a great message. More than this, John recognized his limitations. He understood that his was the work of preparation. His was the work of making straight the way of Another. John knew that he himself must decrease while that Other should in-

crease. Though his message was true, though his mission was mighty, these must come to a close and be eclipsed by Another. John understood that he—was giving himself, all that he was and could do, to make straight Another's way, and to make it possible for that Other to accomplish and achieve.

Than this there is no nobler task, no holier calling, amongst'men, this of making it possible and easy for Christ to come into and be accepted by the lives and hearts of those around about us. Like John, we may help to make His path straight, may call upon those around us to repent, may make it easy for the King to come in and have dominion. In this work all may have a part; John's work is our work yet and in it we may share.

THE OPEN DOORS.

The doors to mission fields are open from both sides, and a returned missionary is quoted as saying that the hinges are off. By both sides we mean that from the homeland side and that on the foreign side; that door here which invites us to enter with our gifts, our prayers, our co-operation, and that door yonder which guarantees access and entrance to the presence and attention of those whom we would reach.

Here Laymen's Missionary Movements, and Men and Religion Movements and kindred activities tell us that the people are entering this open door of opportunity and are becoming interested in increasing numbers in the King's business as it pertains to missions. Business men have seen a great light and are becoming awakened to a great and growing cause. It is coming to be realized that the burden of missions is not a burden at all, but a blessing. As the question is studied and dealt with in its larger aspects this becomes more and more apparent. Missions is one of the great and gracious opportunities God has given man to make him larger, richer and happier. It has taken man a long time to fully realize this, but he has come to it, and is coming to its full realization more and more.

Moreover, the non-Christian world has opened the door, and "taken off the hinges," at the other end of the line. To quote from the returned missionary referred to, "It took ninety-six years to win the first million converts; the next million came in twelve years; and the third million are coming in six years' time. Last year 140,000 members were added to the churches of Christ in non-Christian lands—400 a day, 17 an hour." This may yet seem small; but the ratio of increase is momentous. The outlook

looms large. Results are apparent and exceedingly manifest.

With such facts before us, the people who do not take advantage of the opportunity, enter the open doors, do not deserve to prosper—and under God cannot hope to do so. God has clearly indicated the way. Are we following therein?

GRABBING AT A STRAW.

As to how editors who favor the open saloon and lose no opportunity to take a fling at prohibition, think and write may be judged from the following editorial taken from last Sunday's esteemed Virginian-Pilot:

"Almost coincidently with the time when Dr. Cannon was telling the Virginia legislature how successfully Statewide prohibition operated in North Carolina, Rev. W. L. Davis, head of the Prohibition league in Carolina, was standing on a public platform. in Raleigh exhibiting samples of whiskey which had been. obtained within a few hours from a number of blind tigers in that city. Which witness shall we believe?

"The Raleigh Times, which is not an anti-prohibition paper, pithily says: "We al know that the prohibition law is not enforced in this city." And testimony from impartial sources to the same effect reaches us from many other towns and counties in North Carolina. So that, Dr. Cannon's assertion to the contrary notwithstanding, we are constrained to believe that conditions in Virginia under local option are decidedly better than those in Carolina under State wide interdiction of the liquor trade."

May the angels of mercy defend us. Now isn't there logic and argument for you? We would call that Solomonic, if we really thought our contemporary meant to be serious.

Why man a life, Davis' exhibition of the liquor was no reflection on the law, and the strange thing to us is that any sane and sober men should so consider it. It was a reflection on the indifferent and unconcerned guardians of the law, on a police that blinked and didn't care. If thugs and thieves knock down, drag out and rob at will in Norfolk and the Norfolk police stand on street corners and whistle and sing while the law breakers go on their way unnoticed, unmolested by those chosen to safeguard and enforce the law, we wonder if the esteemed Virginian-Pilot would be consistent and urge the repeal of the law against thugs and thieves? Or would it commend itself to the intelligence of sane people and call on the police and the constabulary to enforce the law?

We wonder if it ever occurred to our

beloved contemporary that there was in this world a difference between a good law, and bad and indifferent guardians of the law?

No, sir, neighbor, we haven't yet heard on any sort of authority but what our law is all right. And what Mr. Davis is after is to show the people in some of our cities that they need to wake up some of their police and to educate the people to the fact that this good law, which the people of the State by more than 40,-000 majority said we want is being openly and flagrantly violated and that their will, expressed at the balot box, is being thwarted by indifferent and unconcerned and exceedingly lax officers of the law.

EDITORIAL COMMENT.
Flagler and Florida.

But for the odium that attaches to his name, because of domestic conduct and the scandals issuing therefrom, Henry W. Flagler's name would go down in Florida's history as one of its greatest benefactors. His work in developing the East coast and in projecting and carrying to success the over sea railway from Miami to Key West is monumental. This railway mostly over water is 156 miles long and has employed an average of 3,000 men nearly ten years in its construction. Where dredging and blasting carol rock made it possible the road is upon great embankments built from beneath to high above the water surface. Enormous bridges span the deep water channels, one of which known as the Flagler Viaduct is seven miles long and is the longest bridge in the world. The road is now complete to Key West and the schedule time from New York to Key West is forty-four hours. A line of ferries carrying entire trains is to operate from Key West to Havana. Monumental indeed. By canals we turn the sea into lands and by dredges and derricks we turn lands into seas, but God is the Creator of them all and by the Word of His mouth, and in the twinkling of an eye, He can bring man's mightiest work to naught.

China A Republic.

Comes interesting news indeed from China on February 12. The Emperor and Empress Dowager (the latter being till now the real ruler of the realm) have issued on this day an edict in which they proclaim that they abdicate the throne which for three centuries their own dynasty has occupied and give way, to a Republican form of government. This from their pen reads more like romance than actual occurrence:

"The majority of the people are in favor of a republic. From the preference of the peoples' hearts the will of heaven is discernible. How could we oppose the desires of millions for the glory of one family?

"Therefore, we, the Dowager Empress and the Emperor, hereby vest the sovereignty of the Chinese Empire in the people.

"Let Yuan Shi Kai organize to the full the powers of the provisional Republican government and confer with the Republicans as to the methods of union assuring peace in public with the union of Manchus, Chinese, Mongols, Mohammedans and Tibetans.

"We, the Empress Dowager and the Emperor, will thus be enabled to live in retirement, free of responsibilities and cares and enjoying without interruption the nation's courteous treatment."

On the other hand the Republic of China—doesn't that sound strange though—agrees to allow these dignitaries to retain their titles, and to be respected as a foreign monarch, to receive an annual grant of $4,000,000 Mexican money, to be allowed to reside within ten miles of Peking and observe the sacrifices at their ancestral tombs and temples, to retain the palace attendants but not allowed to increase the number of eunuchs; the Emperor's private property is to be safe-guarded by soldiers of the Republic.

This of course does not settle the difficulties and dangers in China, but it greatly relieves the situation and gives place for further attempts at peace and government by the people. February 12, 1912, will go down in history as one on which the republican form of government went forward at a mighty bound.

SUNDAY READING.

A minister who was supplying a pulpit not his own was entertained in the home of one of the prominent members of the church. The conditions of the home life impressed him deeply; and although he was careful not to disclose anything that could identify the family, he referred to the Sunday spent in their home as among the dreariest and least profitable in his whole experience.

The family, straggling down to breakfast Sunday morning, brought with them the gossip acquired at various places on Saturday night. Two of them had been to the theater, one had been to a party, most of them had been out late. More than one of the household began the day with a headache.

On the breakfast table there were three Sunday newspapers. On these different members of the family pounced, and were soon hidden behind them.

Only the father and the mother went to church; the young people were "too tired," and did not care to dress.

After the morning service the minister found the newspapers well shaken out and scattered. There was hardly a chair that did not contain one or more parts of one or another of them.

After the Sunday dinner the papers were seized again, and creased and reversed in the weary quest for new sensations.

The home had a good library, but no member of the family opened a boow that day. The library had the poems of Whittier, Lowell, Longfellow and Holmes, as well as those of Shakespeare and Tennyson, but no member of the family read one of them, much less any distinctively religious book.

The hymn book on the piano lay under a trashy song that came with one of the newspapers. The family Bible on the center table was buried deep beneath the so-called "comic supplements."

The whole atmosphere of the home all day was commonplace, worldly and depressing. There was nothing that lifted the thoughts of the members of the family above the tiresome round of the world and the things of the world. Business, politics, scandals and bargains were the themes of conversation. The three secular newspapers, each with its sixty-four pages, covered not only the seats, tables and carpets; they covered the spiritual life of the family as well.

Not questioning the morality of such a Sunday, what may we not say of the pity of it? Is the soul of man so mean, so sordid, that not one hour of one day in the week can be saved for an acquaintance with the better things of litera. ture and of life, and for the higher ministrations of the spirit?—Youth's Companion.

———

—The esteemed Virginian-Pilot, Norfolk, says the oyster ought to be lifted out of politics," but that the thing cannot be done. And it really seems this way from the time consumed every two years by the Virginia legislature wrangling over this very thing. However, if they will send for us and a few other "down homers" of our acquaintance, we will agree to lift our share. We tried it Christmas at several Virginia oyster roasts and found it an exceedingly agreeable task. Command our services, beloved contemporary.

———

No man who is down need fear a fall.

CHRISTIAN CHURCH AT RALEIGH BUILDING FUND.

Dear Readers:

The next issue of The Christian Sun will have an article giving you some definite idea of what is being done by our Raleigh people in the interest of the building fund of the church. All the Mission Boards are interested in the movement and are making appropriations to get such a church in Raleigh as we need. We appeal to all of you to help us in some substantial way. The people are subscribing liberally to our modest call. We feel sure of success, but the question is, How much success do we want as a people in this city? To build a church that will be a credit to our denomination in this great State we will need a great deal more money than we now have in sight. The privilege of giving will be clearly put before our people in and out of Raleigh. We hope all who read The Christian Sun and all who may hear of the work otherwise will make a contribution to the work. God the Father of us all is leading in this campaign and He will not let it fail.

You may fail to do your part, but we are very sure that the plan will not fail. The privilege is yours and you will no doubt do your duty in your response to a call as worthy as this one seems to be. If you are at all interested in our work, write to Chas. H. Stephenson, Sunday school Supt., or to Rev. L. F. Johnson, the pastor, Raleigh, N. C.

THE SUNDAY SCHOOL, THE CHILD, THE FATHER.

(Primary Union Department of the Eastern Virginia Christian Sunday School Convention.—J. H. Blanchard.)

Dear Editor and Readers of The Sun:

The Committee appointed on the Primary work for our Sunday Schools composing the E. V. C. S. S. Convention have for two years made a careful study of and many visits to various schools in our Convention. During the same time we have, each year, prepared a special outline of study for the Primary classes of our various schools to take up without interfering with the regular study of the International lesson, only supplementing the Committee's outline as the conditions of the class work warranted. Some of our schools accomplished much with the studies, drilling the children in various Scriptural texts given in the outlines. Others did not undertake to teach the outline at all. The work done, therefore, has been a help to some schools, also to

the Committee, in helping them to understand more fully what we really need in way of literature in the Primary Department of our Schools. This year we pass out in deeper water and have tried in the best way possible to prepare a more complete help for our schools. We find many helps for the Primary work, yes, many methods and plans, but, to my mind, they are not yet what is needed by our schools to accomplish the two super me difficulties we are now facing: First, not only teaching, but drilling the child in the knowledge of "God Its Father" the fundamental principle of a Christian life and, second—the proper grading of the Department. We do not feel that the literature supplied the schools this year is yet perfected in these particulars, but we do feel that for the ultimate aim of the Committee it surpasses any other material that we have been able to get, and we hope that not long first our publishers will have prepared and published a thorough course to meet the growing needs of our school along the lines mentioned. This course taught and used in the schools as prepared will meet the need in teaching the child its relation to God as its Father and followed will in the course of only two or three years have the school properly graded without any radical change at any stated time, naturally shaping itself as the child is given the next study.

The School.

The following is an extract from the helps prepared for the Primary Teacher by the Committee, under the head of "Forward:"

The greatest need of the Primary Sunday school is better classification, and the greatest need of the Primary scholar a fundamental knowledge of God and the relation which exists between God and child. Primary Union Work, supplemental to the Uniform Lesson, is prepared to meet these ends. How nearly it does this rests with them in whose hands the Work is placed and whose duty it is to present and teach it. In regard to classification, the problem easily solves itself if the outline as laid down is pursued. The Sunday school year should date from July to July (our Convention year) and scholars should be required to pass at this time from one classification to the next higher upon recommendation of teacher approved by Primary Superintendent. Thus all classes will be kept in proper stage and setting for best results in Uniform Lessons as well as Primary Union Work, and the school will become graded gradually, without the objectionable feature of seeming to force an unpopular measure; and, further, the

Work being arranged in continuous or rotary style, the four classes or grades will be a unit all over our Convention.

As to the other purpose of the work, that is, the need of the scholar as stated herein, we have sought through the texts given and their teaching to impress upon beginners the fundamental idea of God and his Son, and then advance that idea in steps best adapted to the child's mental and spiritual development, bringing him at about ten years of age to such understanding of Father, Son, and Spirit, that he will be drawn to the Christian life, and to such knowledge of Bible facts and principles that he may recognize and comprehend his true relation to God, and thus enter God's service intelligently and with a consciousness of personal obligation.

Primary Union lessons are not intended to be co-relative to the International Lessons. They are supplemented, that is take the place of International in whatever degree conditions and characteristics of a class might warrant, and are independent of the themes taught in the uniform course. Primary Union lessons are fundamental, and are co-relative to each other, that is, they take up the study of God and His word to the beginners and follow, at least in an imperfect way, the unfolding of God's truth, bringing into harmony with that truth the child's whole being according to natural and spiritual development. This sort of teaching and knowledge, we think, anybody will admit, is very essential to the religious training of the young and is sadly lacking in the International system of lessons.

The Father.

Some people question the teaching of the Father, Son and Spirit or the Holy Spirit, to Children. Those asking the question do not say that it is, but wonder if this subject be not beyond the comprehension of the grades. We think not, we have been exceedingly cautious in handling this thought. It is not mentioned until the last topic under First Primary, there the topic cited is, "Seek ye first the Kingdom of God and His Righteousness; and all these things shall be added unto you," Matt. 6 33, a text commonly used in winning children for Christ and the topic, "Father, Son and Spirit," second Primary follows. In either instance we think we have used nothing that seven or eight year old children cannot grasp. Besides, in the schools throughout the Convention the average age of the child in these grades is nearer ten. So, we are leading the child toward preparing him for giving his heart to God is the ultimatum of Primary Union, and it was never done yet without the ministrations of the Spirit in some measure. Very true, children have joined the Church without a knowledge of these things. It is here the trouble lies and is the very thing that Primary Union needs to overcome. In short, we have sought to do in this particular, exactly what the last paragraph of the forward says; in other words, to have the child do understandingly what he has done sometimes imitatingly.

DIVISIONS IN CHURCHES.

The history of such divisions is a long and very painful one. Only God himself is able to estimate the harm that has resulted from them. There are churches which, to this very day, are sadly suffering from divisions among them that occurred many years ago. A large variety of things have been causes of such affairs. In many instances, doctrinal differences, between members of the same church have led to most serious divisions. In other instances, a division has been caused by the obstinate and evil leadership of a few men in a church.

One or two officials, destitute of vital piety, have so conducted themselves. as to lead to a bad breach in a church. Men of this type are very likely to have the support of other unconverted members, for such ones draw together. A deceased writer has said: "The quarrels which rend churches are generally the work of two or three stiff-necked, wrong-headed men, who make up in will and won't what they lack in grace. These men, by crafty scheming, draw others to their side. There is, probably, hardly a church quarrel that might not, at one time, have been averted by the absence of a very few worldly-minded and self-willed men, who instigated and accomplished the mischief of which others bear the shame and blame. Sometimes one or two first class funerals will settle a church quarrel that has embroiled the community for years." It is evident from Paul's letters that he had a great dread of divisions in churches. He did everything in his power to prevent them. He most earnestly sought to have the members of churches avoid even the smallest beginning of a division among them. He told them to allow no roots of bitterness to grow in their midst. He was totally against having unconverted people in the church, not only because they were not Christians, but because they would be likely to create disturbances and divisions. He knew that there was no real unity between such ones and true believers. He urged fervent unity between all true Christians, but was positively against a union of believers with unbelievers. And such should

be the case in these days. The very great mistake which many Christian churches are making is that of receiving unconverted ones into membership. They are taking among them the very elements which are apt to cause division and damage to them. Keep your church pure.

C. H. Wetherbe.

Wentworth S. S.

Dear Bro. Editor:

After several Sunday evening disappointments, on account of bad weather, Wentworth Sunday school succeeded last Sunday evening in completing its reorganization for 1912. Without a dissenting voice, Bro. J. L. Sorrell was reelected superintendent. Other officers are: Bro. N. R. Stephenson, assistant superintendent; L. D. Stephenson, secretary and treasurer; the writer leader of music. We now have five classes, two of which are organized: Baraca and Philathea. Bro. J. M. Banks is teacher of the Bible class, Mrs. L. D. Stephenson, the Paper Class, and N. R. Stephenson, the card class.

The Baraca officers are: Brother Nat Overby, president; Bro. Ira Ritchie, vice-president; Crayton Banks, secretary; Jesse Sorrell, treasurer; Leon Stephenson, teacher.

The Philathea officers are: Miss Vivian Atkinson, president; Miss Lella Smith, vice president; Miss Johnny Matthews, secretary; Miss Ida Bell Gill, treasurer; Mrs. G. M. McCullers, teacher; Miss Effie Matthews, assistant teacher.

It has never before been our pleasure to see so much unity manifested in organizing and planning for a year's work in the Sunday school cause.

We cannot doubt but that our Philathea, during their visit to Elon, caught enough of the College "Do things" spirit to put unity, life and spirit in our whole school. At any rate we are moving forward with a visible determination, God being our helper, to do more and better work this year than ever before.

We are exceedingly fortunate in having with us this year Miss Bettie Stephenson, Miss Annie May Cahoon, and Miss Mabel Whitehurst, all of whom have proven themselves skilful and willing workers in the Sunday school cause.

Our C. E. Society is still alive and although the weather was quite cold, we on last Wednesday night had twenty-five members present and received five new members. We are hoping to organize a Teacher-training class at an early date, with Miss Bettie Stephenson in charge.

George M. McCullers.

ELON COLLEGE LETTER.

The interest in the approaching visit of Dr. Frank Samuel Child, non-resident professor of History and Literature, of Fairfield, Ct., is wide-spread and genuine. No lecturer is more heartily received and more thoroughly enjoyed than is he. Ever since his first visit some fifteen years ago he has been a favorite with the successive student bodies and faculties. I can recall how in my student days a prospective visit and a course of lectures by Dr. Child was campus talk for many days. And the old-time fascination of the students for him continues. The reason for this is easy to seek: Dr. Child is himself a student, and always has something to say which is worth while.

There is serious and sympathetic regret, however, that Dr. Child's health at this time is not very good. He has suffered severely in recent months of rheumatism and is not entirely well now. A private note states that he has to hobble around and remain in bed a goodly portion of each day, wrapped in warm blankets. Here is hoping that his annual visit, which we know will be fruitful to us of intellectual and spiritual things, may be to him fruitful of physical improvement and up-build. It is a great pleasure to us that his cultured and accomplished daughter, Miss Bessie, who has been such efficient assistance to her father in his laborious undertakings both in the pastorate and in the literary life, is likely to accompany him on this trip. Dr. Child will deliver two lectures this year and will preach on the first Sunday in March.

This annual visit brings to mind a recent performance of our distinguished friend in a literary way,—the publication of the tenth volume from his eloquent and learned pen,—the title of the book being "A Country Parish," This book, of 251 pages, is handsomely bound and beautifully printed and is brought out by the Pilgrim Press of New York. It is a book that every religious worker should read. Primarily it is a record of the achievements of the parish over which Dr. Child presides, one of the oldest and most influential parishes of New England, antedating by many years the Revolution and numbering among its pastors many of the leaders of action and thought in the country during all these eventful years. But equally is it the glorification of the influence and the setting forth of the place and privilege of power of the country church and pastorate. I wish that every country pastor would read this book and then, realizing the rare opportunities such a pastor has for real leadership, determine to measure up to the full limit of power for such a field of work. Since reading this book, if I were a preacher, it would be difficult to get me to become a city pastor.

If, after reading this volume, you would like to see it all just as it is: if you would like to see a parish with its possibilities realized and with its pastor the center of influence and the dynamo of leadership, not in church affairs in the narrow sense only, but in the religious, social, cultural life of the community as well, just get off the train at Fairfield, Connecticut, investigate that country town and you will see it. What Dr. Staley is to Suffolk, that Dr. Child is to Fairfield. To one who has visited the Old New England town and spent happy hours in the Sherman Parsonage and on the serpentine beach and among the hoary trees of the surrounding forests this book is full of delightful reminiscences and grateful memory. And I am persuaded that all who would like to see the infinite possibilities of the country parish worked out in masterly fashion would do "wisely and well" to acquaint themselves with this interesting, engaging volume.

        W. A. Harper.

NOTES AND PERSONALS.

—Our Raleigh people mean business, and here is wishing them all success in their meritorious undertaking.

—How about getting your neighbor to subscribe for The Christian Sun. This will be a favor to him, a kindness to us and a blessing to yourself.

—We are glad to learn that Dr. P. H. Fleming is recovering rapidly from the effects of his recent arm fracture sustained in falling on the ice.

—We are sending out about 1,500 letters this week to our dear friends. We trust these will have prompt and favorable attention. We think they deserve favorable reply.

—Pastors will you help us increase The Sun subscription list? We need your co-operation, your active assistance now. Have you spoken to your congregation recently about taking the church paper?

—If any subscriber ordered an Annual and has failed to get it the fault is not ours as all orders have been promptly filled. There are a few copies left. For 20 cents we will mail you a copy.

—Dr. J. H. Jowett drives to the point in this fashion "some people confuse the number of appeals they hear with the number of times they give. The very mention of an appeal makes them sweat with rememberance—of their own generosity." Ever see people like that?

—Secretary of State Knox is to go on a friendly visit of five weeks to the Central and South American Republics, Cuba being the first stopping place, the object being to cultivate a more friendly relationship between our own country and those to be visited. Peace making expeditions are the order of the day.

—Prof. W. P. Lawrence of the Chair of English in Elon College delivered a thoughtful, discriminating and comprehensive lecture in thee College chapel Monday evening on the "Short Story, as represented by the writings of O. Henry." The lecture was heard by an appreciative audience and was much enjoyed.

—Rev. W. D. Harward of Newport News was to supply for the pastor at Berkley, Va., First Church last Sunday. This congregation seems fortunate in securing supply every Sunday while their pastor is away seeking health and strength. And good news indeed it is that comes from Asheville that Brother Bryant is improving. A host of dear friends are anxiously praying for this good man's recovery.

—Rev. C. C. Peel has become soliciting agent for The Sun and is working zealously now to help us out in collecting arrearages to The Sun and to increase our subscription list. Any who may aid him in the work will have close and careful attention and will be greatly appreciated not only by him, but by us and by all who are interested in the maintenance and further usefulness of this enterprise of the church.

—What do you think of a business man who gives, not a tenth, but nine tenths of all he makes to church and charity? The New York Observer tells of such a business man in Chicago who makes $100,000 a year, but $90,000 of it he gives to the Lord's cause. The man is happy and prosperous of course. Another man in the same city is told of who gives all his time, but two and a half hours a day, to charitable and benevolent work.

—Perseverance in Christion service ultimately wins out and victory comes. The Biblical Recorder gives a case in point. "Mr. W. C. Pearce tells of a Christian woman who a few years ago tried to start a Bible class in a rough Colorado town. But the cowboys rode in, firing their revolvers and terrorizing all present, Satan's minions seeking to block the Saviour's work. However, the brave woman held on and now in that class she has sixty-seven cowboys, some of whom come on horseback eight miles every Sunday."

—Our good friends, J. Beale Johnson, Mrs. Johnson, and sister, Miss Lena, are whiling away some of these shivering, freezing, snowy days in Florida and of all the cruel kindnesses we have experienced this is the limit. One day it is a card of outing on the bay or gulf, fishing in those teeming waters, the next a scene from orange groves where the fruit hangs luscious and the blossoms are beautiful, the next, wide-spreading lawns, stocked and abundant with green shrubbery and blooming flowers. Only a day's journey away and yet we shiver here with cold and hunger. Why in the world do we not live hard and lay by from our savings during the rest of the year and then take February off—and go to Florida. Mrs. Editor and I have decided to do that soon as all our subscribers voluntarily increase their subscriptions to two dollars a year and all pay up in advance and bills for postage and paper get reduced one-half.

SUFFOLK LETTER.

This winter has militated against church activities and suggests the importance of making best use of good weather when we have it. In fact, weather contains opportunity as well as time and seasons contain opportunity. I have no doubt that God furnishes every person with ample opportunity not only to make his calling and election sure, but ample opportunity to provide for bodily wants; but "procrastination is the thief of time" and we all realize this when cold pinches, hunger gnaws, and despair tortures the soul.

I think much of dumb animals when the temperature drops, the snow falls, and the wind blows. How dependent on man! The wild animals are more capable of providing for themselves than domestic animals. Now, whether this dependence comes from what man does for them, or whether it comes from God's design as man's charge, I do not now suggest; I simply say that man owes the horse, the cow, the hog, the sheep, the mule, the chickens, the dog, etc., shelter against the storm and ample food. His care of these is not only a charge, but good discipline for his soul. Jesus was born in a stall and his gospel owes a debt of gratitude to the manger that housed the Lord when there was no room in the inn. The stable is a good place to show true religion. Many cows may witness against Christians who have neglected them in winters like this. You know Jesus spoke of the stones crying out: if stones could speak, why not dumb beasts?

Every farmer ought to resolve this winter to provide good stalls for his animals before next winter and fill his barn with provender for them. Those long summer days to come will make it possible for all domestic animals to fare well next winter. It is too bad for the horse that hauls the wood to suffer while we sit by a good fire; it is just as bad for the cow to stand. all night in the rain while we eat the butter in a warm dining-room. We shall never treat men right until we treat domestic animals right; for right is tested by how we treat the helpless.

No rest is more sweet than the rest of the man in the country who has "fed up" and left all his animals warm and safe against the cold. His fire glows with new warmth; his bed is like down; the night winds chant praises around his home; his dreams are of angels and peace. The long night adds new strength to his arm, new hope to his heart and new value to his estate, no matter how few his acres nor how small his possessions. The evening prayer of a man like that goes up above the stars that look so cold and far away, for God loves the man who loves life, and it was the lowest life that Jesus came to save.

Miss Mary Foster came to Suffolk to visit Miss Virgie Holland and was taken sick and carried to Lakeview Hospital where she was operated on successfully for apendicitis by Doctors Rawls and Harrell. She is now doing well in convalescence. Her father, John Foster, of Burlington, N. C., came down to see her and worshipped with us the first Sunday in February. Drs. J. E. and D. L. Rawls and D. L. Harrell are making their mark not only in practice, but also in surgery.   W. W. Staley.

NORFOLK LETTER.

The Sunday School Banner was won by Rosemont. It was nineteen per cent. ahead of its nearest competitor. If Rosemont succeeds in winnig the banner for three successive quarters, it becomes its permanent possesion. The award was made for the highest total percentage in collections, gain in numbers, and average attendance. The following is the order of the schools in percentage of gain based on membership of each at beginning of quarter:

Percentage of gain in members—
                                              Per cent.
1 4th Church (Lambert's Pt.) 63
2. First Church (Berkley) 58
3. Rosemont 29
4. Third Church 23
5. South Norfolk 7
6. Memorial Temple 3
7. Portsmouth .... —

Order in Average Attendance.
                                              Per cent.
1. Rosemont 83

2 Third Church 69
3. First Church 62
4. Fourth Church 56
5 Memorial Temple 54
6. South Norfolk 44
7. Portsmouth 41
Collection each person present—
1. Rosemont .... 5.4c.
2. Third Church .... 5.4c.
3. Memorial Temple .... 5 c.
4. Fourth Church .... 4.1c.
5. South Norfolk .... 3.3c.
6. Portsmouth .... 3.3c.
7. First Church .... 2.8c.

Read through the above carefully. There is food for thought and room for improvement. Keep the list for reference and see what happens by April 1st when the new reports will be printed. Five cents per member each Sunday is the standard set. Three schools reached it and two of them surpassed it. Rosemont shows a most remarkable average of attendance. On the basis of 100 members, 82½ (called 83) persons attended the regularly. What other school can show as good a per cent. of attendance? It does not seem to the writer that Portsmouth should be judged wholly by the figures, for they show that of every 100 enrolled 59 remained at home each Sunday during the quarter and only 41 members out of each hundred came. The writer believes this hardly does Portsmouth justice. It probably so appears because persons remaining away were not dropped at the beginning of the quarter. The committee which awards the banner is preparing uniform regulations for all the schools. This may somewhat readjust matters.

Total per cent. of schools—
                                              Per cent.
1. Rosemont 219
2. Fourth Church 200
3. Third Church 200
4. First Church 176
5. Memorial Temple 158
7. Portsmouth 107
(Does not include per cent gain. Not reported).

May the rich blessings of grace from our Father in heaven be upon the superintendents, teachers, and pupils of the schools that their work may lead many into life eternal.

Last Wednesday evening the South Norfolk church elected Bros. J. W. Blassingham, Luther W. Curling, and William J. Curling as deacons to be ordained next Sunday.

Rev. W. H. Garman, the new pastor at the Fourth Church, preached today. We rejoice with Lambert's Point that they have at last obtained a pastor.
                                    A. M. Hanson.

WAS IT A MISTAKE?

As the program is being arranged for the next session of the Southern Christian Convention, our minds naturally go back to the last convention, its program and its work.

The program was largely composed of prepared papers on the various subjects before us. They were both instructive and entertaining, but is it not possible that the work of the convention would have been more practical and also more beneficial to our cause if more time had been used in free and open discussion?

I have no desire to criticize the program committee nor the chairman of the various committees who had the papers prepared, but we all want the convention to be as interesting and helpful as possible and I thought perhaps if we would have fewer papers this year and allow more time for extemporaneous discussion that it might be more helpful since it is better to have the opinion of a half a dozen men on any one subject than that of one, however well it may have been developed. If it was a mistake two years ago, let us avoid it this year. If it was best then, let us follow it now.
                                    W. T. Walters.
Winchester, Va.

WHY TAKE THE CHURCH PAPER?

The primary reason for taking a church paper is the same as for reading general literature—it is for information. Read-ing general literature or secular papers or magazines, however, will not take the place of reading a religious paper or papers. General literature is designed only for general information and culture; but there is a spiritual side, or part, to our nature, and this can be met only by a direct appeal to it through literature prepared especially for it. This is the special function of the religious journal, and no other kind can do its work. A man should take his church paper or papers—in fact, he must take them all, in order to understand his church and its work fully. Our interest goes with our intelligence; and unless we know what is being done by our church benevolent boards, what our churches are doing in the way of building operations, what our people and pastors are doing in the way of evangelization, we cannot have an intelligent interest in our denomination. In a very real sense, the very existence of the denomination depends, in part, upon the circulation of the church papers.—The Methodist Recorder.

Striving to do better, oft we mar what's well.—Shakespeare.

SUNDAY SCHOOLS and CHRISTIAN ENDEAVOR

Edited by Charles A. Hines, Greensboro, N. C., editorial secretary of the Young People's General Convention.

* * * * *

Motto: A Christian Endeavor Society in each Church; Teacher Training and Organized Classes in each Sunday-School.

* * * * *

The secretary will be glad to give any information as to any of the things the convention stands for and where literature can be obtained. Contributions are invited and every class or society should make frequent reports to the above address.

WHY NOT A SOCIETY?

Some Arguments for Christian Endeavor vor Organizations.

Is there a church in the denomination too small for a Christian Endeavor Society? Frankly, I do not believe there is. The best work is not always accomplished in the largest societies, and just as much good proportionate to the number of members may be done in a small organization as a large one.

Many are filled with a desire to do good in the world and to help others but fail to realize that the way to do this is to begin at home. If a young man or young woman has an aspiration for service, he or she can do no better than organize the young people of the community into a band whose purpose will be to save themselves and to save others.

There is work for a society in every community. If you do not believe this, put on your thinking cap and go over some of the needs of the community. Are there no neighbors who do not attend Sunday school and the church; do none of your neighbors ever get sick and if so appreciate flowers and good things to eat? Is there not work needed on the cemetery fence, the church yard or the interior of the church? Above all this is not there a general need of training and developing young men into workers for the Church, the Sunday school and the cause of missions?

If any of the above conditions exist in a community, a Society ought to be instrumental in providing for those things. Then, too, a well conducted Society will give the young people some outlet for their energies. In no other feature of church work is there such an opportunity for young people learning to do the Master's work. Many a young man has offered his first prayer in a Christian Endeavor Society; many a woman can point it out as the place where she sang her first solo.

There will never be a society in your church, if there is none now, until some one starts a movement for one. The one who first suggests it will find that other young people have been thinking of the same thing. Nobody has made a move. There will be no society in the church until some one does make the move. Will you be the one? If a meeting is announced, you will find lots of young people ready to help. It is something they need.

After the society is organized, the work must not be permitted to suffer. Some definite work must be given each to do. Some earnest young man will be glad to build the fires. Another will order the literature. Several will keep the church grounds in order. The girls will provide flowers for every service. Some will lead the meetings. Others will provide special music. A library might be started. Members could buy books and these be put in and exchanged from one to another. Write prominent men and ask them for a book for your library.

Truly you are missing a great deal and losing much opportunity for service if you do not have a society.

NOTES ON C. E. TOPIC, FEB 25.

Subject: The Home Missionary Whose Life Has Most Inspired Me. Acts. 15: 23-35.

Not enough has been said and written of the pioneers of the Cross in America. We have done honor to those men who blazed the trails for gold-seekers and land-seekers, but many of the names that have figured in the onward march of Christianity have not been handed down to posterity crowned with the glory that is theirs. Truly we may expect that many men and women whose names are unknown to us now are on the honor roll in heaven, and some day we shall hear of their service, sacrifice, toils, sufferings and victories. It will be sweet indeed to hear the Master say to them, "Well done, thou good and faithful servant." The wives of these men in many instances, have borne just as heroic a part in the struggle for Christ's kingdom and they too, shall reap with them the crowns of glory.

The Christian Endeavor World has collected some notes on the soldiers of the Cross in America, which are appended:

John Eliot, the apostle to the Indians, was driven from England under the rule of Archbishop Laud, and settled at Roxbury, Mass. His spirit was stirred by seeing the ignorance of the Indians, and he devoted himself to their uplift. He established among the people the arts of peace. In his tours he endured many

hardships. "I have not been dry," he says, "night or day from the third day of the week until the sixth, but have traveled from place to place in that condition; and at night I pull off my boots, wring my stockings and on with them again, and so continue." David Brainerd, born at Haddam, Conn., in 1718, lost his father and mother in childhood. At an early age he became concerned, he tells us, about his soul, which destroyed his eagerness for play. With rare courage and marvelous consecration he devoted his life to the Indians. His bed at times was a bundle of straw placed on boards. He had to send ten or fifteen miles for the bread he ate, and then it was often mouldy and sour. Pastorates were offered him, but he clung to the Indians. There he saw the greater need. His life illustrates, among other virtues, the love that a white man can have for races of another color.

The story of a number of Indians coming to St. Louis to ask for the white man's Book stirred the conscience of the East in the early years of last century. Leaders of thought determined that gospel should be sent to those Indian tribes; but who should carry it? To undertake seh a mission required no ordinary courage. Jason Lee was ready; however, to respond to the call. Accompanied by his nephew he went west to what at that time was no man's land. In 1834 the two men crossed the Alleghanies. On July 27, 1834, Lee preached the first sermon ever preached west of the Rocky Mountains. He pushed on to Vancouver, settling finally, however, in Oregon, a pioneer of the cross, ready to suffer all to carry the white man's Book to needy people.

The story of Marcus Whitman, which every schoolboy knows, inspires with its lesson of dogged determination to achieve the impossible. On this journey to the unknown West he was accompanied by his bride, making the trip one of the strangest honeymoons on record. On July 4, 1836, the travelers had crossed the last crest of the Rockies. They unfurled the American flag, knelt in prayer, and dedicated to God the vast Oregon country. Whitman's famous ride eastward, across the continent, is in keeping with the character of the man; a soul undismayed at difficulties, a soul burning to do good in his field, for his country.

President Roosevelt speaks of Samuel Doak in his "Winning of the West." Doak came from New Jersey. He was educated at Princeton. Filled with the pioneer spirit, he walked through Maryland and Virginia, driving before him an old flea-bitten horse loaded with a sackful of books. He crossed the Alleghenies and came down along blazed trails to the Holston settlements. He founded the first church in that cradle-spot of Tennessee, a log house built near Jonesboro in 1777. He built the first log high school, which developed into Washington College, the first educational institution in the Southwest. Doak is only a type. Many others like him put their courage and valor and learning and consecration into the building of our nation.

Aratus Kent was a successful pastor in the East, but the apostolic spirit which long for new fields to conquer stirred within him. He heard the cry of the West. When the need of thousands of miners and merchants living on the shores of the Upper Mississippi, without church or school were put before him, he responded, "I go." Twenty-seven days after leaving New York he landed at Galena. The following day being Sunday, he gathered a congregation in the dining-room of the hotel, and there began the first preaching of the gospel in northern Illinois. The nearest church was two hundred miles distant. He visited every village and settlement for hundreds of miles around Galena. He laid the foundation of three colleges and two ladies' seminaries, which exist today. The conquest of the land for Christ would not be far distant if all Christians possessed the spirit of Aratus Kent.

The study of heroic lives will enable us to live nobler and not to yield to what is low and selfish in our own natures. It is a great encouragement to any struggling soul that others have passed through the same fiery trials and come out victorious in the end.

Faith is the victory that overcomes the world. The strength of temptation is in the lust of the eye, the lust of the flesh, and the pride of life, and because all these are so attractive, millions yield to their blandishments, but faith discovers for us the highest good, the beauty and strength of spiritual life and so we endure as seeing the invisible.

America—all America. Is there a fairer field? Is there a broader field, where prospects of success are more favorable? Is there a field more providentially located than this one today? Can we be saved, if we fail to recognize our opportunity, and hence, our obligation, in this matter? Can the world be saved, and the great commission be fulfilled, if America is not Christianized? There are many within this territory who are not Christians, and there are many who, though they hold church membership, nevertheless need Christianizing.

TREASURER'S REPORT.

Rev. L. I. Cox, Elon College, treasurer of the Young People's General Convention, reports the following payments received since the last report:

Mrs. Jas. L. Foster $1.00
Orphanage C. E. 1.00
Rev. W. G. Clements 1.00
                                    ———
Total $3.00

NOTICE! NOTICE! NOTICE! TO ALL PASTORS AND SUPERINTENDENTS OF ALL S. S. IN THE SOUTHERN CHRISTIAN CONVENTION.

The following resolutions relating to our Teacher Training Department, have been adopted by the Sunday School Committee of the Southern Christian Convention:

"RESOLVED:"

Third: That we adopt an enrollment card and record file, as per samples exhibited by the chairman, for his use and he is hereby instructed to purchase the same.

"Fourth: That we operate our Teacher Training system and general Sunday school policies in harmony with the International Sunday school movement. That we purchase a seal to be attached to all certificates and diplomas issued by the International Sunday School Association to teachers and members of the (Rev. McD. Howsare was authorized and requested to purchase this seal for the Committee.)

"Sixth: That, inasmuch as the Christian Publishing Association, through its Board of Trustees has announced "Preparation for Teaching," by Oliver, to be the Elementary, or First Standard Course, recommended to our church; and inasmuch as Dr. McElfresh, International Teacher Training Supt., commends this work in highest terms; we acknowledge this book as such and adopt it as the

Elementary, or First Standard Course of the S. C. C." (Signed:)
                              H. E. Rountree, Chmn.,
                              M. W. Butler, Secretary,
                              L. F. Johnson,
                              J. W. Manning,
                              McD. Howsare.

This means that we are now prepared to enroll systematically all Teacher Training pupils of our Sunday schools, both those who are now pursuing the course and those who may at any future time undertake it. I have the enrollment cards and also the record cards, and a nearly perfect system of keeping them. I expect to have the file at some early date. I want to call your attention to the

First Standard Course.

It has been said that the Advanced Standard by Prof. Harper and others is too heavy and hard for the average Sunday school worker. We have adopted "Preparation for Teaching," by Oliver, not merely to be in harmony with the Christian Publishing Association, but because the work is meritorious, concise and comprehensive and suitable to the mind of the average Sunday School teacher and senior pupil. This book may be secured by applying to The Christian Publishing Association, Dayton, Ohio, or The Christian Sun, Elon College, N. C.

How to Secure a Diploma.

We have decided that the best plan is the International, and we will act wisely to submit our work to them for recognition. We will conduct this department under our own official supervision, but each enrollment will he duplicated in the same Department of the State Sunday School Association. Whenever a class or an individual finishes satisfactorily the Elementary or First Standard Course, the International Diploma will be issued bearing the seal of our church (See resolution No. 4). Examinations may begiven by sections, but statement of grades only will be given for these. The diploma will be given upon application and satisfactory completion of the book.

The Advanced Standard.

Special official Certificates will be issued to students who satisfactorily complete any full section or text-book of an Advanced Standard Course. Upon a satisfactory completion of the Course we will issue the beautiful lithographed Advanced Standard Diploma (large size) of the International Association, our seal attached.

We wish to enroll during the present year a class in every school. Wherever a class is impracticable the "Individual plan" serves well. We desire to make it so that a willing teacher may have no cause or excuse to be untrained and unprepared.

Now there is this much about it,—a fact of which we cannot rid ourselves: We owe to the rising generation a trained teachership. We owe to the future church trained workers. We owe to God the responsibility of our opportunities provided by Him, and we owe Him our best service. The Committee will do its best to inaugurate this department to successful operation. If you will respond to our pleas even as well as you can, be it ever so little, we shall have great success.

Watch for further articles on this subject. H. E. Rountree, Chairman.

ELON COLLEGE NOTES.

Tonight in the College Chapel Prof. W. P. Lawrence will deliver a lecture on The Short Story, taking O. Henry as its chief representative.

On last Saturday evening the executive committee of the N. C. Christian Endeavor Society met in called session in the President's office here, Dr. R. E. Steele, presiding. The committee selected the city of Raleigh and the First Christian Church of that city as the next meeting place of the State Union, but the exact time was not set, some time in April, however, being most favored. The members of the committee present were Miss Florence Ledbetter, Dover, N. C., Dr. R. E. Steele, Lumberton, and Profs. Amick and Harper.

The Publication Board of the Southern Christian Convention will meet here Tuesday night. Important business will come up before this committee, and announcement of their work will be made later.

Mr. C. B. Riddle, who has been occupying the position of business manager of The Christian Sun office has resigned his position on account of heavy college work, and he has been succeeded by Rev. C. C. Peel of this city.

Mr. G. H. Whitley, a prominent lawyer of Smithfield, Va., and a member of the class of '92, spent Sunday with his nieces, Misses Virgie and Janie Lee Beale, and other friends.

Prof. T. C. Amick occupied the college pulpit yesterday and preached a most excellent sermon.

Mrs. Griffin, of Chapel Hill, spent Sunday with her sister, Miss Affie Griffin, a popular teacher in the Graded Schools.

The lumber and masonry are being collected for the immediate construction of the new porch at West Dormitory.

Miss Mary Lou Pitt was a pleasant visitor at the home of her friend Miss Jennie Lashley on Saturday and Sunday. On Sunday, Miss Pitt sang in the Presbyterain church of Mebane.

We are glad to note that Rev. M. L. Bryant, who has been ill at Asheville, N. C., is improving rapidly. His wife has taken a position in the city schools of Asheville, in order to be near him.

On the night of the 22nd of February, the Clio Literary Society will render its annual public entertainment. And following this entertainment there will be served in West Dormitory Dining Hall, a banquet in honor of the old, active, and honorary members who are here. Quite a number of alumni and old students are expected to attend this banquet and it will be made the occasion of a reunion. The program of the entertainment is as follows: Violin Solo by Mr. J. M. Manry. Oration entitled, "Winning the Race," by Mr. W. A. Trivette. He will be followed by Mr. O. M. Barnes with a humorous selection. Mr. John L. Farmer will then, in an oration, discuss "The Other McNamaras," after which Mr. Orlando Barnes will render a Bass Solo. The chief item of interest, however, will be the debate, which has resolved itself into this: Resolved, that raw material, essential to subsequent manufacture, should be free from custom duties on entering the United States. Messrs. Henry C. Southard and C. B. Riddle will champion the Affirmative, while the Negative will be upheld by Mr. C. C. Ward and Mr. K. W. Loftin. Mr. J. A. Dickey, Jr., will preside and Mr. J. F. Parsons will act as secretary. The marshalls who will look after the audience are Messrs. H. P. Cline, Jr., J. A. Woods, and Robert E. Lincoln.

A letter from Rev. G. O. Lankford announces the fact that his wife who has been seriously ill for some weeks is steadily improving.

Dr. Frank S. Child, Fairfield, Conn., will arrive on the Hill the very last of this month. Dr. Child always has in store for us something good and we are confident that he will bring us this year

messages which will do us good. The exact program of his lectures and their subjects has not yet been announced.

A. L. L.

BELIEF AND UNBELIEF.

(Among unpublished manuscripts of N. Summerbell I find matter much like the following:)

Religion is an acknowledged element in the nature of man.

All nations, tribes and peoples have been religious: the Babylonians, Egyptians, Canaanits, Greeks, Romans, Indians, all. That which is natural and universal must be designed to be satisfied by the Creator. Otherwise, one might say that God gives appetite, but does not intend to satisfy it with food; he gives eyes, but does not make them useful by creating light; he gives intellect, but does not meet its capacity for development by making knowledge possible.

Man sacrifices the present for the future, and looks from earth to heaven. He is a moral being, has a consciousness of right and wrong, which the brute does not have. Man bends the knee in devotion, he worships, he sings praises to God, he prays to his heavenly Father, and he worships the unseen; which the brute does not.

Man is a being of illimitable progress, growing from a condition of nakedness, soon clothed with skins, to a state of refined civilization, sending news around the world, through air or under the ocean; but the brute is the same as 6,000 years ago, whether lion, eagle, robin, or honey-bee.

As religion belongs not to brutes, but to intellectual beings, it cultivates the intellect, builds temples of science, schools and colleges. There are hundreds of academies, colleges and universities all over Christendom; but none built by brutes. And there are none built by skeptics, who regard themselves only as developed brutes, unless with funds furnished by others, either directly or indirectly. Where sacrifices are made for education it is always by religious people. And schools where genuine scholarship is permanently promoted are always the product of religious impulse, or of religious families. The infidel community is usually as adverse to education as to morality. Loafers are not usually Christians educated. Education belongs to the religious inhabitants of the earth. Brutes are not religious.

Brutes pursue with avidity the calls of nature, to supply the wants of the body; but man by thought traces causes to effects, and effects to causes. The brute sees the watch, the statue, the ship, the ears; but seems to have no thought of the maker. Man thinks of the mechanic, the architect, the builder.

So the atheist sees the world and its adaptations, but he has no God. He sees the laboratory, but not the Chemist; the locomotive, but not the Engineer; the sun, moon and stars, but no Creator. Religion belongs exclusively to the moral part of creation. As there can be no mortality, or sense of conscience in brutes, so in the cultivated brute (the atheist), there can be no religion. The brute cares only for the present world and the present wants; and so the atheist is carnal. But the true man, the man of intellect, lays up treasures in heaven. True men and angels are alike in various things. Both are religious; they adore God; they love virtue and religion they have a home in heaven; they love wisdom, benevolence, mercy, truth and God. They regard themselves as immortal, or as living for immortality, commencing an existence never to end.

But the atheist differs from genuine men and angels in all these things. The brute worships no God; and the atheist does not. The brute sees no heaven above the sky; and the atheist does not. The brute never bows in prayer; and the atheist does not. The brute expects no reward for virtue; and the atheist does not. The brute has no well defined rule of virtue and the atheist has none. The brute discards marriage; and so does the atheist. The brute has no immortality in view; nor has the atheist.

If God should awaken the atheist, or materialist,, in this world, or the world to come, he would say—Now I leave the grade of brutes, and rise to the plane of angels, or men.

The mass of learned men are Christians: Copernicus, Kepler, Galileo, Newton, Bason, Agassiz, Hitchcock, Whittier, Longfellow, Bancroft, Motley, Orton.

Religion includes three grand elements: faith in God and his word; desire of holiness and worship; longing for immortality. The brute and the materialist do not have these things. * * * Go by night and view the stars and drive unbelief away; indulge the rising hope of everlasting day. * * * How short is life, and how narrow its province, compared with the possibilities of eternity, with everlasting improvement of mind and virtue, in the constant approach of God.

Man viewed aside from religion is an insoluble mystery. He has more cares than the brute; with no adequate reward for any of them except the physical, if materialism, or atheism, be true.

Man's body and human passions are animal. He eats, sleeps, works, fights, loves, hates, as an animal. He is provided with two hands for helps, feet for walking a stomach for food, and an un-

right form. But his body is unprotected, and apart from his divine reason, though beautiful, he would be comparatively helpless; his skin is shielded by warm fur; his feet not hardened, like hoofs. He cannot fly like the eagle, swim like the fish, run like the antelope, or defend himself like the lion. But yet, on account of reason, he is the master of all things. He weighs evidence, plans enterprises, examines the animals, investigates himself, and searches God.

The materialist who flatly denies honesty, virtue, charity, mercy, and the graces of religion, startles us with a doubt of his moral health; and we consider him only a brute in human form, and doubt his word in a court of justice.

Reason asks the materialist to account for the origin of life, the variety of forms, the adaptations of need, supply, and mystery of death. For if mere nature gives and sustains life, why does not life continue to increase? The nourishment which causes growth would continue youth, would renew the body, and death. If matter were self-existent, its evolutions would be so; and the same nourishment which causes growth would continue it with increasing life and power; and nothing but the want of supply could cause death. Thus, from the materialistic view, death is as much a mystery, as life.

A lady of wit made a party, where a coxcomb became disagreeable by his infidel remarks. Being reproved, he said that he was sorry that in a gathering of intelligence and beauty he alone had the honor of not believing in God. The lady replied. "You have not that honor alone; my dog and cat share it with you."

J. J. Summerbell.

THOSE WHO GUARD THE POPE.

The most singular and striking body of trained soldiers serving under any potentate is that which garrisons the pope's palace in Rome. From the silver-casqued Noble Guards, the Swiss Halbordiers in doublet and ruff, down to the Palatine Guards in shako and the Pontifical Gendarmes in bearskin, they form a distinctive feature of the papal court and a befitting setting to a mediaeval picture. Their gorgeous or quaint uniforms, glancing helmets, flashing arms, glittering breastplates—the black velvet doublets, ruffs and rapiers of the gentlemen-in-waiting—are in perfect artistic harmony with their surroundings, from which they receive and on which they bestow that correlative fitness of the Vatican, although the presence of these troopers and foreign mercenaries, morally speaking, is an anomaly and an anachronism.

This singular little army of soldier-

potentate consists of noble Roman volunteers, burgher civic guards and Italian or foreign mercenaries, and comprises four companies, differently armed, uniformed and officered, and each possessing a distinct history of its own and a separate organization.

First in dignity and antiquity come the Noble Guards, in their scarlet tunics, golden epaulets and silver helmets. Raised in 1485 under the name of Light Horsemen, they were formed into two squadrons; many years later, in 1555, their strength was increased by the addition of 100 free lances, chosen exclusively from the scions of noble houses who could show a sufficient number of quarterings. The two corps were re-organized and united into one by Pope Pius VII in 1801, when, after the stress and storm of the great French revolution, he had righted the ship of St. Peter. These noble guardsmen mount guard in the antechamber of his holiness' private apartment, and escort the pope when he drives out. They now number 69 all told, under the command of a lieutenant-general.

The Swiss Guards, who rank next in precedence, were first enrolled by the fighting Pope Julius II and subsequently, during the 17th and 18th centuries, three companies were added to the original one. After many vicissitudes, they were finally reduced to one company, which musters 122 men of all ranks, commanded by a captain ranking as colonel. The other two corps of household troops—namely the Palatine or Palace Guards and Pontifical Gendarmes—are far more modern, and do not possess the same stirring traditions. They are chiefly employed in church ceremonies, conjointly with the gendarmes, to maintain order among the crowds who throng St. Peter's on such an occasion; and they are called out about once a month to drill or to mount guard. They number 170 men of all ranks, and are all volunteers, providing their own uniform and receiving a small annual allowance for incidental expenses.

The Pontifical Gendarmes—though last in precedence, by no means the least in appearance of the four pontifical corps—were raised in 1816 to replace the French military police instituted by Napoleon I and, like the Irish military constabulary, were charged with the protection of persons and property throughout the whole papal states. Reduced in numbers and duties, they now muster but 96 men and officers, and perform police duties within the Vatican at state ceremonies, as on the occasion of the present Pope's jubilee, and act in conjunction with the Palatine Guards in keeping order within St. Peter's—Ex. The head of a church guarded in a fashion like

THE CHRISTIAN ORPHANAGE.

Rev. Jas. L. Foster, Editor, Elon College.

Officers of the Orphanage.
.as. L. Foster, Supt., Elon College, N. C.
J. O. Atkinson, Chr. Board of Trustees, Elon College, N. C.
O. L. Barnes, Treas., Elon College, N. C.

Amount brought forward ....·$50.69

Dues.

John Newman Denton	.10
S. E. Denton	.10
Joseph Rabb Denton	.10
Mary Lee Foster	.30
James L. Foster	.30

Monthly Offering.

Henderson, N. C.	2.61
Franklin, Va.	5.26
Morrisville, N. C.	1.65
Mt. Carmel, Va.	1.00
Philatheas, Pleasant Hill	.35
Spring Hill, Virginia	3.00
Catawba Springs, N. C.	2.75
Hines' Chapel	1.53

Special Offering.

Pope's Chapel, N. C.	5.00
S. C. Hobby, Raleigh	50.00
"A Friend," Franklin, Va.	.50
Chas. D. Johnson, Graham	5.00
Zion, N. C.	4.50
Sanford, N. C, Ch., & S. S.	7.48
Mrs. A. F. Iseley	.30
Mr. and Mrs. C. Iseley	1.00
S. S. Class, Ansonia, O.	5.00
Sale of 2 calves	5.66
Catawba Springs, N. C.	4.00
Concord, N. C.	1.00
Amount 2nd week, 1912	$108.49
Total	$159.18

Elon College, N. C., Feb. 7th, 1912.
My Dear Children and Friends:

Our second week presents a very nice report, and we are grateful for the same, though we are sorry that so few cousins have letters in. You see these Thanksgiving offerings continue to come in. We are glad to have such a nice number of Sunday schools to begin reporting for 1912; and we hope that all schools will do the same and that many will obligate to feed and clothe a child for this year. Also church and friends are requested to send us five dollars or six for the feeding and clothing of a child 1912?

We are deeply grateful to Bro. Hobby of Raleigh for his liberal annual gift to the Orphanage. For a number of years he has kindly donated to our support.

Hoping that there may be many who will join the number who support a child, and also that there may be quite a few who will be one of 20 to give $50.00 each for the payment of our $1000.00 mortgage indebtedness by April 1st 1912. Write me.   Uncle Jim.

McRae, Ga., Jan. 31, 1912.
Dear Uncle Jim:

Time flies so fast since Santa brought us new playthings. And, too, we are busy flying kites with the big boys now that we have strong winds. Love and dimes.
                    John Newman Denton,
                    S. E. Denton, Jr.,
                    Joseph Rabb Denton.

March is with you early, children. Our boys are thinking of baseball and have already played with another team and beat. They feel greatly encouraged.

Dear Cousins:

We are away behind with our dues, but send 60 cents to pay up for 1911. It is very easy to get behind and we don't mean to let it be the case again. We children here at the Orphanage will be glad to see warm weather. We have been housed so long it will be a treat when we can get out of doors and play "Blackman" again.   Lovingly,
                    Mary Lee Foster,
                    James L. Foster, Jr.

HAVE YOU A BLIND BABY?

Until a few years ago there was no institution fully equipped for the care, maintenance and education of the baby blind. But now there is an exceptionally fine one, known as the Arthur Home for Blind Babies, on Pinegrove Avenue. Summit, N. J. It is a large stone building, with Nursery, Hospital, Home and Kindergarten departments.

There are 25 children there already. The Kindergarten teachers are graduates. The Hospital Department is headed with one of the best graduate nurses to be found, with trained nurses; the Hospital staff is composed of the best surgeons and doctors of the country.

The Institution is maintained by the International Sunshine Society, the largest philanthropic newspaper club in the world. Headquarters, 96 Fifth Avenue, New York City, N. Y. Originally all the members were newspaper writers, but since the dues are only kind deeds, the ranks have been joined by good people from all parts of the country. These newspaper workers discovered there was no provision for blind babies; that they were put in the Poor Houses of the different counties, or sent to the Idiot De-partments or Institutions for Feeble Minded.

Mrs. Cynthia Westover Alden, a newspaper writer and editor, is the President of this Society, and rightfully maintains that we have no right to assume that a child has no brains because it is blind. The Society has proven that if proper care and training is given, the baby will grow up into a beautiful normal health-loving child, with the exception that it has no eyesight. The Society took the so-branded idiots and feeble minded from the different states, put them in the Institution and gave them the best care and training that could be secured, and has proved the truth of Mrs. Alden's statement, for out of eighty-two children supposed to be beyond all help, only two failed to respond to the training.

It has also been discovered that the mortality among the blind babies is something alarming. The light hunger is greater than that of food, and the blind babies, instead of sucking their thumbs, dig their little fingers into the eyes and rub for the light (that never comes) until the eye is injured, and as a result often blood poisoning sets in and the baby dies.

When the Summit Home was opened, of the thirty-one children on the list when the workers began to prepare the Home, only one could be found.

Not one of the children now in the Home was on the list for admission when the Home was opened.

Love and money will not save a blind baby's mind. The very mother-love that hugs the baby closer and closer to her, is the greatest enemy the child can have. Daily, the mother will see her baby grow more feeble right under her eyes. It takes a graduate nurse to carry out the doctor's orders as to its physical care, and it takes a graduate kindergartener to train the mind that should be trained daily, yes, hourly. The mother can no more save her blind baby from becoming feeble in mind than she can give it a college education and do her other duties at the same time.

If you know of a blind baby, tell the parents of this institution, where it can be sent and be saved from growing up feeble in mind and crippled physically.

Letters directed to Mrs. Cynthia Westover Alden, 96 Fifth Avenue, New York City, President-General, International Sunshine Society, or to Mrs. Kate Coleman, Superintendent of the grove Avenue. Summit, N. J., will receive prompt attention.

"Get the best out of each day that you can and soon the black clouds will fade away and life will be worth living."

MARRIED.

Gay-Raiford.

At Mr. West's, 205 Penner St., Suffolk, Va., Jan. 16th, 1912, Mr. Carlton Gay and Miss Fannie Belle Raiford, both of Mt. Carmel church. The happy young couple have the congratulations of their many friends.   H. H. B.

Holland-Shaw.

At number 207 Chestnut St., Suffolk, Va., Jan. 24th, 1912, Mr. James E. Holland, telegraph operator at Myrtle, Va., and Miss Sallie Ethel Shaw, of N. C., The happy young couple took the Southern Ry. for Charlotte, N. C., and Southern cities. They have the congratulations of their many friends.   H. H. B.

Owens-Orndorff.

At the parsonage on January 25, 1912, I united in marriage Mr. Richard Owens and Miss Arabella Orndorff, both of Frederick County, Virginia. The groom is a farmer by trade. The writer's best wishes follow them.

           W. T. Walters.

Boyce-Foreman.

Mr. Herman M. Boyce and Miss Lena B. Foreman were quietly married at the parsonage on the evening of January the 18th. May their lives be long and happy.

           W. T. Walters.

DIED.

Thomas.

Mrs. Maggie Watson Thomas was born September 19th, 1849, in Moore County, N. C., and died January 21st, 1912. Age, 62 years, 4 months, and 2 days. She married William A Thomas, March 19, 1874. To this union were born three sons and two daughters, Bert W., William L., and Malcom C., Mrs. Clemmie B. Thomas and Mrs. Mary L. Hunt, all of whom survive her except Sister Hunt, who died about 18 months ago. She was converted in early life and joined Shallow Ford Church, of which church she remained a loyal and faithful member till death.

Sister Thomas was on of the most humble and unassuming Christian women I have ever known. I say it to her memory that in the years I have known her and served as her pastor she treated me more like my own mother treated me than like a stranger.

Her life was one of simple and sincere faith in God. A kind word, a gentle deed, a sympathetic tear on her cheek was all the demonstration she ever made: but you could feel her sympathy and friendship. She leaves a devoted husband, four children, five grand children, and a large

circle of kinspeople and friends to mourn their loss. The burial services were conducted from Shallow Well Church in the present of an overflowing house. The grave also was covered with beautiful flowers wrom friends and loyed ones. The services by the writer, assisted by Rev. G. R. Underwood.

           Jas. L. Foster.

Griffin.

At the home of her daughter, Mrs. J. E. Baines, near Cypress Chapel, Nansemond County, Virginia, January 15th, 1912, Mrs. Lucy Griffin, relict of the late Abram Griffin, aged 94 years and 8 days. She was the oldest member of Cypress Chapel church. She made a profession of religion when very young and united with the church and was truly one among the best Christian mothers and grandmothers that it has been my privilege to know. On one occasion when I was in her home after prayer she clasped her hands and said, "Bless the Lord," and threw her arms around her husband's neck. They were both over 80 years of age then, and said "God bless your dear old soul. We have been living together over fifty years, and you never gave me a cross word in all your life." Uncle Abram preceded her some years to the better land. Dear Aunt Lucy has been waiting and watching for some time for the angel to come and take her to see and be with her many loved ones again. She leaves one son, Mr. Jesse Griffin, of N. C., one daughter, Mrs. Jas. E. Bainees, of Cypress Chapel, Va., 20 grand children, and 17 great grand children, also a host of friends. She has been living the most of her time, since the death of Uncle Abram, with her grand daughter, whom she reared, Mrs. A. H. Wilkins, of Cypress Chapel, Va. Her funeral services were conducted by her pastor at the church and her remains were laid to rest beside those of her husband in the church cemetery. God bless and comfort the dear bereaved ones.   H. H. B.

Eley.

At Ivor, Virginia, Jan. 25, 1912, Mr. and Mrs. George Eley's only child, little Oscar M. Eley, aged one year, one month and about 12 days. He was a bright and interesting little fellow and the pride of the home. Jesus said "Suffer the little children to come unto me, and forbid them not; for of such is the kingdom of God." The funeral service was conducted at Mt. Carmel Christian Church by pastor and the remains of the little one were laid to rest in the church cemetery. The dear parents have the sympathy of their many friends.   H. H. B.

Snyder.

Mary J. Snyder was born May 19, 1837 and died Jan. 11, 1912, aged 74 years, 7 months and 22 days. Deceased was preceded to the grave by her husband, who died about 19 years ago, and by seven children. She is survived by three brothers, one sister, and by one son, with whom she made her home. She was a sister of Rev. William A. Dofflemyre, who during his life time was a prominent minister among the churches of what was then the Virginia Central Conference, now a part of the Virginia Valley Central. Sister Snyder united with the Christian Church at about the age of 16, and remained a faithful member until death called her to her reward. Funeral services were conducted by the writer at old St. Peter's Church on the morning of January 13, and the remains were laid to rest in the adjoining churchyard.

           A. W. Andes.

Hammer.

Walter Tate Hammer, so of Rev. M. E. Hammer, was born April 13, 1909, and died Jan. 30, 1912. He had been sick only a few days before his death, and his almost sudden departure came as a severe shock to his family—especially to his father, this being the youngest child. He was buried in the cemetery at Pleasant Grove, near the grave of his mother, who died about two years ago. He leaves an aged grand-father, John Lowdermilk, a father, step-mother, eleven half-brothers, and sisters to mourn his early departure. Christianity assures them that it is well with his soul. The funeral was conducted by the writer.   T. E. White.

Georgia O. Anderson departed this life Jan. 30th; age, 24 years. Funeral services were conducted by the writer at Timber Ridge Christian Church and interment was made in the cemetery adjoining. She was a member of the Disciples' Church at Ebenezer, Frederick Co., Va. She leaves a large circle of relatives and friends to mourn her loss. May God bless and comfort the bereaved.

           W. T. Walters.

NOTICE!

The attention of the Women's Missionary Societies in the E. Va. Conference is called to the fact that Mrs. W. H. Dick, Suffolk, Va., is treasurer of the Conference Woman's Home and Foreign Missionary Board. As stated in the constitution, the treasurers of local societies should report quarterly to the treasurer of the Conference Board.

         Margaret H. Brickhouse,

           Sec. E. Va. Conf. Board

ALONG THE CHURCHES.

...'. Our city has been stirred by a 10 days'
...nion .revival service conducted by Rev.
.. Wm. Black of Charlotte, N. C.
All protestant ministers of the town
took part in these services. There was
a large number of conversions. Every
church had some accessions. We received six yesterday and expect more to join
later.
... The weather has been very cold since
Christmas. The temperature a part of
the time being as much as 16 to 20 de-
grees below zero. But in spite of this,
the interest in our services has been good.
Twenty-two have joined our Sunday-
school since January the first. Jan. 20th
we had 71 present, which is the highest
record in attendance. We are planning
to enlarge the scope of our Sunday-school
work.
Pray that the Lord may lead us to
higher and larger work in His name.
. . . . . . W. F. Walters.
Winchester, Va., Feb. 5, 1912.

Big Oak.

The first Sunday in this month I filled
my regular appointment at this church.
I have preached here three times since
conference. The last two appointments
were on very cold days in addition to
wind and snow. However, congregations
were very good, and we enjoyed the services. This is the writer's home church,
and of course it is a very dear place to
him.
We were made glad on last Sunday
morning when we found some fresh lumber on the church yard which was brought
for the purpose of repairing the church.
The good people have decided to have a
better church building, and have gone
right to work in order to bring it about.
Our plans are to add ten feet to the
length of the church, re-weatherboard
the old part, put in a recess pulpit, and
paint the church. There will also be some
improvements made on the inside of the
church, such as carpeting the floor, etc.
This is one of the most important points
in the Western Conference and we earnestly request the prayers of the brother-
hood in behalf of the work here.
. . . J. F. Morgan, Pastor.

Pierson, Cal., a suburb of Los Ange-
les is, as far as we know, the only city
in the United States without a church of
any kind of denomination. It recently
...

THE LESSON ON THE VALUE OF THE DENOMINATIONAL PAPER.

The Western Christian Advocate of
January 31, 1912, contained an article
written by a Methodist pastor which il-
lustrated so clearly and forcibly the value to the church of the denominational
organ that we surrender to it some of
our editorial space. It is better than any
editorial we can write on the subject.
Here it is:
"In the winter of 1885, while pastor
in one of the county capitals of Ohio,
a sweeping revival broke out in my
church. Among the converts was a young
man of more than ordinary ability, and
a son of one of the families of the
church: As the meetings progressed the
church doors were opened from time to
time, and for some time after the meetings closed. But while others came and
joined, this young man held back. I
asked him why he did so. He answered
that he was not yet ready. I told him I
had expected him to be one of the first
to come, judging from his natural good
sense and honesty as a convert. He smil-
ed and thanked me for my estimate of
him, and assured me that he had no in-
tention of staying out of the church. I
gave an opportunity to join the next
Sunday; and while several came forward,
this young man was not even at the service. The thing worried me, and I went
the next day to the office where he was
employed to have it out with him and
find out the why of the delay. He was
in the employ of an insurance agent, who
was a member of the English Lutheran
Church, who always kept his church paper in his office, where at leisure mo-
ments he might pick it up and post himself on the doings of his church or pe-
ruse it for other religious information.
And this young man had been reading
the same paper. So when I put the m
ter squarely to him about joining the
church, he gave me a jolting surprise by
saying: 'I have concluded to go into the
English Lutheran Church. I have been
reading about it, and I see as a Church
it is doing great things for the Lord, and
that is the kind of church I want to
join.' So the secret was out. He had
been reading an English Luthern Church
paper, but had not seen a Methodist pe-
riodical for the reason that the family of
which he was a worthy son never had tak-
en one of the church papers. I said to
him: 'F—, have you pledged yourself to
join that church yet?' 'No,' said he;
'I attended the service last Sunday.'
... ...'...' if you have
... ... yet I get hold of
... ...' . . .

... you were converted.' And he
... id. I then went home and
... up an armful of the New York,
the Northern, and the Western Christian Advocates, with several copies of
Zion's Herald and the 'Methodist Year-
book.' I carried them to him. I told
him that he need not return them, for
they were all his to keep and study at
his leisure. I then told him that I left
it all with him now, and that after he
had carefully canvassed the matter it
was for him to decide where he would
mke his church home.
"About a week or ten days after we
met on the street. As he approached
me he said: 'Are you going to open the
doors of the church next Sunday?' I
said I would. 'Well,' said he, 'I'll be
there to join. And put my name down
for the Advocate.' I said: 'Good!'
'Why,' he said, 'the Methodist Church
is the biggest and most active religious
institution under the sun, and I'm going
to be in it.' He came unto the church
the following Sunday, and was soon put
into the official ranks, where he proved
to be a most capable and useful brother.
For most of the time he managed the
finances of the church, and every service found him presnt unless sick or ab-
sent from the city. He lived a useful,
happy Christian life, and was a brother
beloved by all. He remained a reader of
the Advocate until he died. His may be
one case out of many where the church
is in danger of losing the children of its
own households because the parents do
not supply the family with the literature
of their church. A very little self-deni-
al along the line of some unnecessary
extravagance will make the Advocate a
weekly visitor in the home."
On one hand, a religious newspaper
came very near to making one a Lutheran who was naturally expected to be a
Methodist. On the other hand, it did
make a Methodist of one who had already determined to be a Lutheran. In
either case the unique power of th newspaper was shown. It is a solemn lesson
here for the pastor and Christian parents.—Nashville Advocate.

"IS MY NAME WRITTEN THERE?"

This is an important and personal
question. When a Christian congregation sings this song, each singer should
put to his own soul this searching inquiry. Each may judge himself. No one
may judge his neighbor, or say to his
brother, "Your name is written on the
... ... ge of the book of God's kingdom."
... ... "My name is written
... ... ay t is honestly, intel-
... ... That assurance

may we have that our own names are in the book of life?

"Is my name written there?"' No one can answer this question affirmatively who does not earnestly desire to have his name inscribed among those who are being saved. No man ever entered into. the kingdom of heaven against his will. No one ever stumbled through the narrow gate by accident. There is a way, a narrow but plain way. It is the King's highway. The very first thing to be noted in this inquiry about the way of life is an earnest desire. Do I long to be saved? This is a hopeful sign, for all such longings are the work of the Spirit of God. "It is God that worketh in you." "Wilt thou be made whole?" "How answereth thou?"

If your name is written there you have surrendered your life to God. So long as we continue to resist the Spirit of God and fight against Him, it is vain to hope. No one can be saved so long as he is set on having his own way. "We have turned every one to his own way." This is the charge in the indictment. It may not be the way of the drunkard or the thief or the murderer or the prodigal. It may not be what the world would call a base, low, beastly way. It may be quite respectable and fashionable and decent. It is not God's way. It is our own way. We never can walk with God until we give up our own way and choose His way. "As high as the heaven is above the earth, so high are my ways above your ways, saith the Lord." He cannot come down to our way. It is too low for Him. He has sent His own Son to lift us up to His way. "Let the wicked forsake his way." Give up your way. Surrender your life to God. Follow where He leads.

All those who make this definite and full surrender to God may claim their inheritance among the saints in light. It is their right in Jesus Christ. He is the way. The man whose life is fully surrendered to God may come boldly into the Kingdom without the slightest fear of being cast out on any account . He may be as sure that his name is written there as if he had seen it with his own eyes. Let him believe it with his whole heart without other evidence than the Word of God. "By grace ye are saved through faith."

Then shall the believer realize that it is indeed God that worketh in him. He shall be conscious of God. "Hope maketh not ashamed because the love of God is shed abroad in our hearts by the Holy Ghost." If the love of God is shed abroad in my heart, I know that my name is written there.

Faith and assurance are constant com-

panions. "Thou wilt keep him in perfect peace whose mind is stayed on thee, because he trusteth in thee." Faith does not always spring up in the soul suddenly and full grown. The disciples, conscious of their infirmity, prayed their Master, saying, "Lord, increase our faith." A certain poet, describing the development of faith in some believers, at one stage of the process, breaks forth with this trembling note, "I then began hoping that Jesus was mine." The darkness had passed. The sun began to shine, but not in its full glory. It was not noonday but morning twilight. The soul began with a wish and proceeded as far as a faint hope. Another step and he sings more clearly, more sweetly, more confidently:

O mercy surprising, he saves even me; Thy portion forever, he says, I will be. On His promise I'm resting, assurance divine,

I'm hoping no longer, I know he is mine. "The path of the just is as the shining light that shineth more and more unto the perfect day."—N. Y. Advocate.

THE CHRISTIAN SUN.

Founded 1844 by Elder Daniel W. Ker
Organ of the Southern Christian Convention.

Entered as second-class matter at the
post-office at Greensboro, N. C.

Printed every Wednesday.   Terms of
Subscription.

One Year - - - - - - - $1.50
Six Months - - - - - - .75
Four Months - - - - - - .50

J. O. Atkinson, Editor, Elon College, N. C.

The Office of Publication is Greensboro,
N. C., 302½ S. Elm St. The Editorial
Office is at Elon College, N. C., as hereto-
fore, to which office all communications
for the editor should be directed.

RALEIGH & SOUTHPORT RY. CO.
Southbound Daily.

STATIONS	A.M.	P.M.	P.M.
v. Raleigh	8:00	1:15	6:35
Caraleigh	8:10	1:23	6:45
McCullers	8:35	1:43	7:07
Willow Springs	8:52	1:55	7:23
Varina	9:04	2:05	7:35
Fuquay Springs	9:14	2:12	7:45
Chalybeate	9:35	2:30	8:00
Kipling	9:40	2:35	8:05
Cape Fear	9:53	2:46	8:18
Lillington	10:00	2:53	8:25
Harnett	10:08	3:01	8:33
Bunlevel	10:14	3:06	8:38
Linden	10:23	3:15	8:48
Lane	10:34	3:25	8:59
Slocomb	10:39	3:30	9:04
Fayetteville	11:10	4:00	9:35

Northbound Daily.

	A.M.	P.M.	P.M.
Fayetteville	8:00	1:00	5:10
Slocomb	8:23	1:28	5:38
Lane	8:33	1:32	5:43
Linden	8:45	1:43	5:54
Bunlevel	8:55	1:52	6:03
Harnett	9:01	1:58	6:09
Lillington	9:11	2:08	6:20
Cape Fear	9:16	2:13	6:26
Kipling	9:28	2:24	6:43
Chalybeate	9:35	2:30	6:49
Fuquay Springs	9:50	2:45	7:05
Varina	10:00	2:52	7:14
Willow Springs	10:09	3:02	7:25
McCullers	10:22	3:15	7:41
Caraleigh	10:40	3:35	8:06
Raleigh	10:50	3:45	8:20
	A.M.	P.M.	P.M.

J. A. MILLS, Supt.
Raleigh, N. C.

he has kindly donated to our ——
Hoping that there may be many who

B. A. SELLARS & SONS,
High Class Dry-Goods

AND GENTS' CLOTHIERS AND TAILORING MERCHANTS.

MAIN STREET. . . . . BURLINGTON, N. C.

ELON COLLEGE (Co-educational).

THE ONLY INSTITUTION of higher education fostered by the Southern Christian Convention.

MODERN IN EQUIPMENT, Steam Heat, Electric Lights, Baths, Sewerage, Ele-
gant New Buildings.

FOUR DEGREE COURSES. Special Courses for Teachers, approved and en-
dorsed by the State Superintendent of Public Instruction and by the County
Superintendents.

A HIGH GRADE INSTITUTION whose graduates are admitted to the graduate
departments of all the great American Universities without examination.

MAINTAINS EXCELLENT MUSIC, Art, Elocution, Normal, and Preparatory
Departments.

A FACULTY OF THIRTEEN SPECIALISTS, with a successful record of twenty-
one years behind it.

HAS ALL THE ADVANTAGES of city life with none of its disadvantages. Sit-
uated in the delightful hill country of North Carolina, famed for its health-
fulness, pure water, and high moral tone.

ELON COLLEGE HAS DONE MORE to build up the Christian Church than any
institution ever yet commissioned by our people.

TERMS VERY MODERATE. $132 to $187 per session of ten school months.
For catalogue or other information, address,

PRESIDENT W. A. HARPER, ELON COLLEGE, N. C.

FREEMAN DRUG CO., DEALERS IN DRUGS,

Medicines, Patent Medicines, and Druggist sundries, Perfumery, all popular
odors, Toilet and fancy articles, Combs, Brushes, etc.
Prescriptions Carefully Compounded.

Burlington, N. C.

Huntley Stockton-Hill Company,
FURNITURE—UNDERTAKERS—SLATE VAULTS.
GREENSBORO, N. C.

Free booklet of vital interest—Farm
demonstration work; Farming for profit;
The best plan known for reduction of
acreage, diversification and rotation; the
best improved farm seeds; earliest, most
prolific and largest yield Cotton; the
proof—not more claims. Send name and
address to Sugar Loaf Farm, Youngsville,
N. C.

—Dr. J. D. McAllister, general Secretary of the Anti-Saloon League of the
State of Virginia, says that whether the
present Legislature shall pass a prohibition law for the State or not, the liquor traffic in that State is doomed and
't another two years will suffice to close
up every saloon in the State. Let us
hope that Dr. McAlister is a true proph-
et.

Terent countries, or ——

—We were pleased to have a visit from
the college, and to our home for the night,
from Rev. A. B. Kendall and wife, of
Burlington, last Friday. We are not sur-
prised that our Burlington congregation
is more than pleased with the work their
new pastor is doing, and the assistance
rendered him in his work by his excellent
wife. Bro. Kendall is an able preacher
and a most likable man. He captured
Elon folks with his sweet gospel message
and he will be heard here with gladness
whenever he can come.

CHRISTIAN SCIENCE.

Some people think a pain's a pain'
But Mother's sure it isn't;
And Grandma smiles and says her aches
Must be the reumatism't.
—January Woman's Home Companion.